Isabelle Graw

Three Cases of Value Reflection: Ponge, Whitten, Banksy

AF622998

Institut für Kunstkritik
Frankfurt am Main
Isabelle Graw
Daniel Birnbaum

Isabelle Graw

Three Cases of Value Reflection: Ponge, Whitten, Banksy

Sternberg Press

Preface

This book considers three cases of artistic production in terms of value reflection: namely, the writing of Francis Ponge and specific artworks by both Jack Whitten and Banksy. Value in artistic production is presupposed as something the latter can actually reflect upon. Before examining this argument in greater detail, I will clarify the notion of value that guided my thoughts. For a start, I assume artworks are ontologically split between having what Pierre Bourdieu called their "symbolic" and "market" values, although I consider this divide to be less absolute.[1] Whereas Bourdieu argued for a strong polarity between these two forms of value in his analysis of the French literary field in the late nineteenth century, I consider the two forms as interrelating and pointing to each other. This interrelation manifests in values that cannot be fixed and need to be constantly renegotiated. One could illustrate this dynamic interrelation between symbolic and market value by looking at artworks in the market sphere for which symbolic value (such as recognition from curators or writers) is an absolute prerequisite for their market value. But the opposite is also true: there have been many artworks with little or no symbolic value (meaning that, for instance, a renowned art critic didn't write about them) that have nevertheless managed to reach high market values (e.g., prices) at auction.

This gap between symbolic value and market value can also occur with artworks that possess cultural importance—a symbolic value that doesn't necessarily translate into market

1 For more on this, see my essay "Market Value and Symbolic Value," in *High Price: Art Between the Market and Celebrity Culture* (Berlin: Sternberg Press, 2010), 31–33.

values (or if it does, only after a long period of time). Apart from values ascribed to artworks from the outside, I also focus on another (seemingly more substantial) notion of value that applies once artworks circulate as commodities, namely, their "commodity Value," a term I have borrowed from Karl Marx's labor theory of value.[2] I propose to retain the fundamental character of this value by treating this word with a capital *V*. According to Marx, commodity Value is both founded in labor and abstracted from it; thus, its origin in concrete human labor is obscured. However, I propose that commodity Value takes on a special form when occurring in artworks, which is why it needs to be conceptualized differently. Artworks do resemble commodities in some respects—they circulate in the value sphere, for instance, and they equally depend on labor (although artistic labor naturally differs from wage labor). But apart from these structural similarities, art commodities are also commodities of a special kind, since unlike ordinary commodities they are *unique* material products that are closely bound to their singular author (via a signature) and his or her artistic labor. Instead of obscuring human labor, as done with ordinary commodities, artworks have the capacity to suggest that the specific artistic labor that has been expended *for* them is somewhat present *in* them. Now, this idea of an absent artistic labor becoming present (or graspable) in artworks is of course a fantasy, but one that artworks are nevertheless able to nourish and materially substantiate since traces of this labor are often visible.

2 See Karl Marx, "Commodity and Money," in *Capital*, vol. 1, *The Process of Production of Capital*, ed. Frederick Engels, trans. Samuel Moore and Edward Aveling (London: Lawrence & Wishart, 1996), 45.

Some scholars have argued against the notion of artistic labor as being special or exceptional, rightly pointing to the increasing similarities between artistic and general labor in recent years.[3] Indeed, "creative subjects" are omnipresent in the working world of today, and artists are more and more expected to "manage" their careers or to "invest" in their futures. But despite structural overlaps between artistic and general labor, I would nevertheless argue that the former still enjoys specific privileges; for instance, artistic labor appears to be more self-determined, especially when compared to the labor of the so-called creative worker.[4] While there can be no doubt that artists are increasingly exposed to manifold economic constraints (such as tight budgets for production or collectors who request huge discounts on artworks) in a neoliberal economy, they still enjoy privileges and freedoms. Think only of their ability to determine the aesthetic means and purposes of their work, or how the final work belongs to them, at least until it is sold. These are privileges and freedoms of which a creative worker can only dream. Moreover, these residual freedoms associated with artistic labor resonate in the specific commodity Value of artworks. Indeed, this Value manages to appear as something intrinsic—an illusion, certainly, but one that artworks are particularly able to justify, whether materially or through the specific interventions they make in their respective contexts. The widespread belief in art's substantial value can be traced back to the specific characteristics of the art commodity: its uniqueness, its material dimensions, and the fact

3 See Marina Vishmidt, *Speculation as a Mode of Production: Forms of Value Subjectivity in Art and Capital* (Leiden: Brill, 2018).

4 See my essay "Working Hard for What? The Value of Artistic Labor and the Products That Result from It," in *The Value of Critique: Exploring the Interrelations of Value, Critique, and Artistic Labour*, ed. Isabelle Graw and Christoph Menke (Frankfurt am Main: Campus Verlag, 2019), 155–61.

that it stems from an artistic labor that is a comparatively privileged form of labor.

Once we have distinguished different values, between external values like symbolic and market value, and have understood how artworks are defined by their commodity Value when circulating as commodities, the question remains: How can artworks actually reflect on themselves? How can they reflect on something that they are also defined by? This seems particularly difficult considering that artworks are not reflecting subjects—unlike subjects, they can't reflect on their values independently. But what artworks can do is produce value-reflective statements, provided that there is a viewer or interpreter willing to decipher them. Value reflection is thus not an objective quality to be found in artworks; rather, it is an epistemological *potential* that can be claimed for artworks by viewers. This claim requires a certain degree of imagination or a willingness to project on behalf of the viewer. Her claim that an artwork is value reflective can of course be disputed and rejected. When I propose to read the works of Ponge, Whitten, and Banksy as value reflective, I aim to contribute to a discussion that may lead to objections and disagreements.

Now of course the question arises as to why I selected three male artists—a postwar writer and two visual artists from different generations (Jack Whitten was born in 1939 and Banksy, supposedly, in 1974). I certainly didn't intend to present value reflection as a male territory, although it is historically true that the making of a value-reflective artwork often requires a secure social position that allows artists to afford it, quite literally. Many female artists throughout the twentieth and twenty-first centuries, such as Lee Lozano, Andrea Fraser, and Annette Kelm, have produced value-reflective works. My choice of Ponge, Whitten, and Banksy was not motivated by gender considerations but by the contingencies surrounding my own work, including exhibitions seen and methodological and aesthetic turns that have occurred in my writing and directed me toward these practices. But there is another, more substantial reason I chose these artists: to my mind, each of their practices displays an exemplary type of value reflection. For instance, Ponge's "doubly materialist" approach both to "things" and to his own material conditions managed to shed light on the spheres of value in which he operated. He analyzed the way his own words produce symbolic value for artworks, and he considered those financial considerations and economic exchanges in which he himself was implicated and that reigned in his social field. Whitten's practice, by contrast, shows value reflection to be inherent in his artistic procedure. The dedicatory character of his memorial paintings, for instance, turns them into "gifts" (to other artists or musicians). Through their status as gifts, they are part of an exchange and thus enter into a perpetual economic cycle. Compared to Ponge's playful invocations of his own financial conditions, Whitten's value reflection is more indirect and procedural. It is the latter's decidedly material and semiotic practice that situates his works into a specific value sphere (the Western canon) that traditionally excluded Black artists like him. By locating their practice in a system of exchange neither Whitten nor Ponge seems to hope for a place beyond the value sphere, a place that seems imaginary at best in today's capitalism. In contrast, Banksy aimed to destroy the symbolic and market values of his work *Girl with Balloon* (2006), which was shred during an auction at Sotheby's in October 2018. Paradoxically, this act took place in the heart of the art world's value sphere. Not surprisingly, his seemingly destructive attack on symbolic and market forms of value ended up strengthening both: his work was treated like an icon by some institutions, and its price increased considerably following the auction-event. Banksy's intervention demonstrates how "subversive" acts of individual artists are welcome; cultural capitalism tends to applaud and encourage them. Consequently, *Girl with Balloon*, which was renamed *Love Is in the Bin*, didn't manage to shatter the art world's belief in the intrinsic value of art. On the contrary, one could argue that Banksy's act demonstrated once again how commodity Value is able to expand and integrate even those artistic attempts that seek to destroy it.

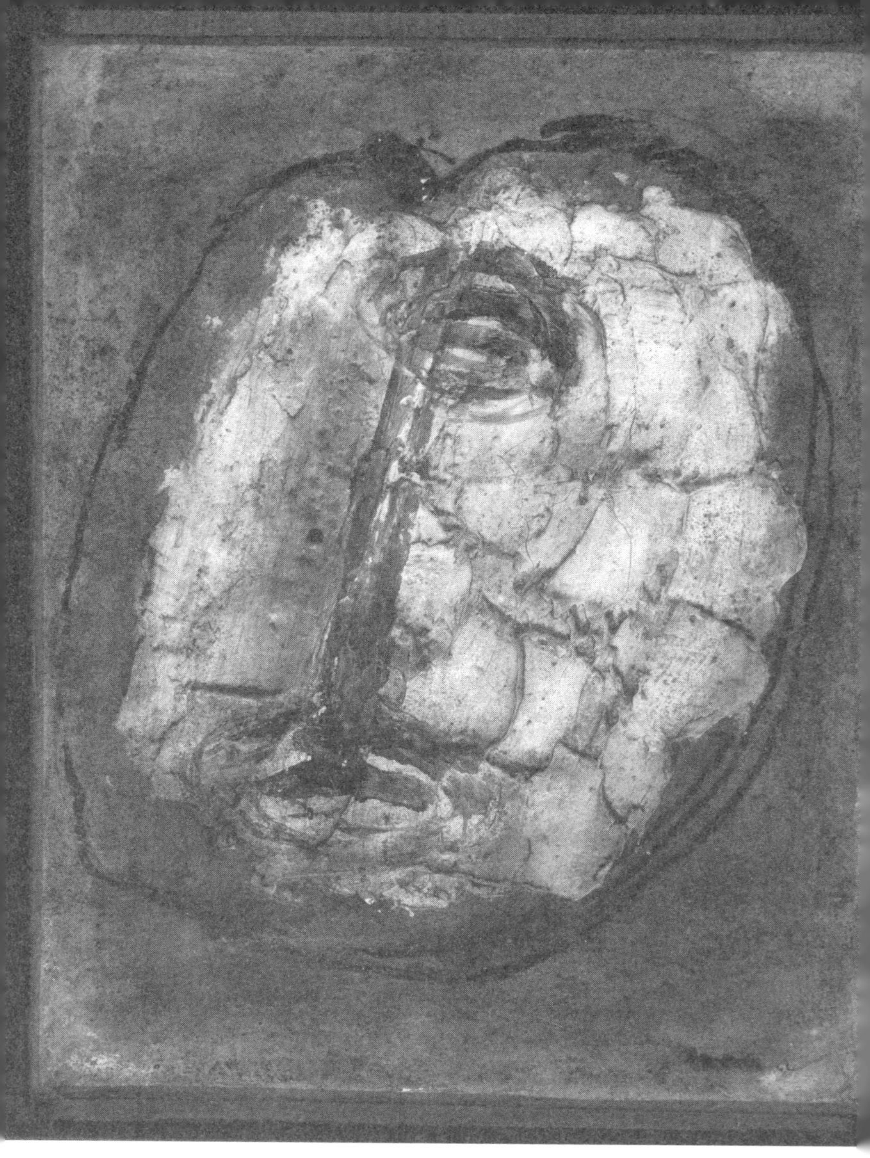

Jean Fautrier, *Tete d'Otage no. 1*, 1944

Ponge and Us
For a Doubly Materialist Art Criticism

Prelude

Francis Ponge's first essay on art, "Note sur 'les Otages,' peintures de Fautrier" (Notes on the "Hostages" by Fautrier, 1945),[1] is not a work of criticism, a review, or a meta-critical essay; rather, it could be described as an elliptical poetic attempt to write about an artist's work. Originally written for the catalogue that accompanied a 1945 exhibition at Galerie René Drouin, which comprised a series of paintings and sculptures by Jean Fautrier that were known collectively as "Les Otages" (1943–45) this text ended up not being used (one by André Malraux was selected instead).[2] Nevertheless, Ponge's essay was later published as a separate book by Éditions Seghers in 1945.[3]

In his writing on Fautrier, Ponge managed to do something that is rare in art criticism: he reflected on its own material conditions by hinting at the financial motivations behind the writing of the text, while simultanenously capturing the specific materiality of Fautrier's paintings by discussing their texture in detail. The text is thus doubly materialist in that it reveals his own material circumstances and describes the physical object. The historical focus of the text—the Second

1 The writings of Francis Ponge (1899–1988) have yet to be translated into English. All quotations in this essay are translated by the author and refer to the German version, Francis Ponge, "Bemerkungen zu den 'Geiseln' von Fautrier," in *Texte zur Kunst*, trans. Gerhard M. Neumann and Werner Spies (Frankfurt am Main: Suhrkamp, 1990).

2 See Yve-Alain Bois, "The Falling Trapeze," in *Jean Fautrier, 1898–1964*, ed. Curtis L. Carter and Karen K. Butler (New Haven, CT: Yale University Press, 2002), 57.

3 See Karen K. Butler, "Fautrier's First Critics: André Malraux, Jean Paulhan, and Francis Ponge," in Carter and Butler, *Jean Fautrier*, 48.

World War primarily, and more specifically war crimes—resonate quite strongly; for example, Ponge described Fautrier's "Hostages" paintings, with their pastel-colored, thick *haute pâte* (matter painting) constructed surfaces, as "puffy faces" and "tortured profiles."[4] Such an anthropomorphic perception of Fautrier's paintings points to their context of creation: they refer to the torture and execution of victims by Nazis that took place in the woods near the artist's studio in Châtenay-Malabry outside Paris.[5]

Uncovering Material Conditions

In his text, Ponge wondered why painters like Fautrier would ask him to write about their work. In an attempt to answer this, he noted that "painters, or their dealers, seem to want nothing more than for their paintings to give rise to words."[6] Painters *and* their dealers are set up here as interchangeable. One can replace the other because they have the same aim: they both want the work to be written about. The result of this proximity between painters and dealers is that the former is then situated within the sphere of capitalist production. Ponge looked at painters without illusions: alongside their dealers, painters operate within the art market, within the sphere of capitalist production that seeks profit above all else. In methodological terms, his text shows the popularity of Marxist thinking among French intellectuals after the Second World War. Like many of his collegues, Ponge was involved in the French Communist Party until 1947. It was his affiliation

4 See Ponge, "Bemerkungen zu den 'Geiseln' von Fautrier," 30.

5 See Curtis L. Carter, "Fautrier's Fortunes: A Paradox of Success and Ponge," in Carter and Butler, *Jean Fautrier*, 20.

6 See Ponge, "Bemerkungen zu den 'Geiseln' von Fautrier," 17. I have analyzed this sentence at length in the chapter "The Economy of Painting: Reflections on the Particular Value Form of the Painted Canvas," which was published in my book *The Love of Painting: Genealogy of a Success Medium* (Berlin: Sternberg Press, 2018), 317.

with Marxist positions that even led to a falling out with his friend Albert Camus.[7] The historical-materialist credo that one's own conditions of production should be rendered *transparent* resonates throughout Ponge's reflections on Fautrier.[8] By stating, for instance, that such writing on "our artist friend […] should bring us a little bit of money (very useful, money, if only to allow us to write other things, writing of another sort),"[9] he sheds light on the financial considerations that probably prompted him to write the text in the first place. But the playful mention of financial gain also disrupts monocausal explanations: his reasons for taking on this assignment were not only financial ones. Ponge did, however, allude to the fact that commissioned work afforded him the freedom to "write other things," namely, his more experimental literary writings about seemingly banal objects, such as a shell.[10] Accepting certain jobs often enables the freedom to carry out more personal pursuits.

As payment, Fautrier supposedly gave Ponge "one or two paintings."[11] This exchange shows the different financial values given to writing and painting. While paintings can potentially attain high market values, writing often doesn't. More so: by referring to the paintings he supposedly received as payment in kind, Ponge also pointed to a widespread practice in the art world, which is often done but rarely spoken about—a

7 See Albert Camus and Francis Ponge, *Correspondance, 1941–1957* (Paris: Éditions Gallimard, 2013), 85, 91.

8 Jacques Derrida already noted Ponge's tendency to hide "nothing of his ideology, his politics, his economy." Jacques Derrida, *Signéponge/Signsponge*, trans. Richard Rand (New York: Columbia University Press, 1984), 22.

9 See Ponge, "Bemerkungen zu den 'Geiseln' von Fautrier," 20.

10 See Francis Ponge, "Notizen für eine Muschel," in *Im Namen der Dinge*, trans. Gerd Henninger (Berlin: Surhkamp, 2017), 7–63.

11 Ponge, "Bemerkungen zu den 'Geiseln' von Fautrier," 20.

practice that was more common at that time than it is today. Ponge referred to "writer friends of the artist" who "took paintings home and kept them there for a while."[12] This type of exchange (loans, gifts, or payment in kind) between artists and writers is depicted here as happening regularly. This casual exchange is also mentioned in Fautrier's correspondence with his friend Jean Paulhan, a writer who wrote on Fautrier's work and who introduced him to Ponge.[13] In one of his letters to Paulhan, Fautrier asked him to choose his favorite painting or drawing in exchange for a piece of writing.[14] Fautrier's request indicates how writers were situated at the top of the cultural hierarchy in the French art world of the 1940s. Writing was considered to possess more symbolic value than paintings—a situation that is of course hard to imagine nowadays, where the opposite tends to be true: writers and art critics in particular are often treated like the poor relatives of their much wealthier painter friends.

But Ponge also suggested the difficulties that result from such exchanges. He presented himself as the (probably fictive) owner of Fautrier's paintings, which were supposedly called *R. L.* and *M. P.* Considering that his own writing might one day help to increase the value of Fautrier's paintings (and thus of the paintings in his possession), Ponge touched on the idea that he was implicated in processes of financial speculation. And instead of hiding any conflicts of interest, which is what most critics and art writers would do today, Ponge wrote about

12 Ponge, 19.

13 Paulhan had actually suggested that Ponge should write the text on Fautrier's paintings. He was the one who arranged their first meeting: "I met Ponge, he is quite alright and thanks to you we spent quite a successful day together." Fautrier to Paulhan, end of October 1944, in Jean Paulhan, *Fautrier* (Bern: Verlag Gachnang & Springer, 2004), 93.

14 Fautrier to Ponge, 102.

them. Financial subtexts repeatedly appear in his writings as well as in his book on "writerly practices," where he also described "material contingencies," such as the financial considerations that prompted him to write the book.[15] Although allusions to financial motives that we often encounter in his work are always staged and literalized, they have to be taken with a grain of salt. It is not Ponge's authentic material conditions that are exposed in his texts; rather, by hinting to financial matters, it is their impact on his work that is at least symbolically acknowledged.

Criticism as Value Generating

In a further attempt to answer why painters like Fautrier wanted him to write about their work, Ponge proposed that it is *words* that make people believe in painting's aesthetic worth: "Good paintings," he noted, "are those that are discussed; the more words, the bigger the audience."[16] Now this kind of ratio certainly doesn't apply today: words—and especially words by art critics—are rarely powerful enough to reach large audiences. But Ponge was also right when he argued that words provide meaning and credibility for artworks: they generate symbolic value that is not intrinsic to the artwork. The symbolic value of an artwork needs to be described as a "social relation" (and this is true for Value in general, as Karl Marx already knew).[17] Symbolic value therefore depends, among other things, on communication.

15 Francis Ponge, *Schreibpraktiken oder Die stetige Unfertigkeit* (Munich: Carl Hanser Verlag, 1988), 32.

16 Ponge, "Bemerkungen zu den 'Geiseln' von Fautrier," 17–18.

17 See chapter 1 of Karl Marx, *Capital*, vol. 1 (London: J. M. Dent & Sons, 1930).

While exposing great faith in the power of words, Ponge also conceded that one could say "nothing satisfactory" about "good paintings."[18] It is the old topos of painting's irreducibility and the resulting impossibility for words to grasp their essence. While acknowledging that his words legitimized Fautrier's paintings, Ponge was skeptical that his writing was on the same level as these paintings. The difficulties invoked here occur because the meaning of paintings is suggested and withdrawn at the same time—a contradictorary double movement that Ponge seems to register. Ponge believed in the exceptional value of painting; exceptional in that it supposedly can't be evaluated. This assumption that a painting can't be fully grasped through words is of course an old mythical trope. But in Ponge's case, it is also based on the writer's experience when encountering the work: he often reminds us how his efforts to grasp Fautrier's paintings are also futile. Ponge probably realized while writing on Fautrier's paintings that to a reader, he could only give an approximated rather than a fixed meaning.

Thinglike Words That Presuppose Subjects

Ponge's approach to paintings (and his other areas of interest) shares some features with new materialism, a rather heterogenous discursive field that conceptualizes matter as being active and powerful. But Ponge's approach to painting also differs from this line of thought in manifold ways.[19] Similar to most adherents of new materialism, he paid close attention to material objects and even gave them a kind of agency. When writing about snails, for instance, he noted that they carry

18 Ponge, "Bemerkungen zu den 'Geiseln' von Fautrier," 17.

19 See Diana Coole and Samantha Frost, "Introducing the New Materialisms," in *New Materialisms: Ontology, Agency, and Politics*, ed. Coole and Frost (Durham, NC: Duke University Press, 2010), 1–43.

around their shells without complaint and described them as content quasi-human beings without self-pity. But unlike new materialism, Ponge didn't underestimate the power of the beholder; his or her presence is always acknowledged. In his notes on a pebble, he constantly referred to the difficulties he had trying to define it. And when trying to describe and relate to a shrimp through his writing, Ponge remains equally present.[20] Even though he claims a quasi-human standpoint for the things he described, he never lets us forget that they can only become alive if someone (like him) brings them to life.[21] Things are thus treated as if they had feelings or intentions of their own, when in fact such human capacities are projected onto them by someone.

It was Jean-Paul Sartre who first noted the persistence of a strong subject in objects that are described as alive and powerful in Ponge's work.[22] Sartre proposed that Ponge couldn't get away from discussing humans, because the world he described presupposes human beings. But despite this latent humanism in Ponge's writing, Sartre also insisted that Ponge aimed to overcome the subject and to replace subjects with objects. The human factor is thus both acknowledged and fought against in Ponge's writing. And the tension captured by Sartre—a tension between things that are subject-like and a subject who grants subjecthood to them—is missing in new

20 Ponge, "Schnecke," "Der Kieselstein," and "Die Garnele," in *Im Namen der Dinge*, 19, 97, and 75–79.

21 Jacques Derrida hinted to the fact that Ponge did both: returning to the "thing itself" like a phenomenologist and projecting "human meanings (psychological, subjective, etc.) onto things." Derrida, *Signéponge/Signsponge*, 12.

22 See Jean-Paul Sartre, "Der Mensch und die Dinge," in Francis Ponge, *Einführung in den Kieselstein und andere Texte*, ed. Christoph Schwerin (Frankfurt am Main: S. Fischer Verlag, 1986), 256.

materialism, which notoriously underestimates the power of projecting subjects that is necessary for objects to appear as possessing agency.

From an art-historical point of view, Ponge's approach to things owed a lot to the Surrealist method of *écriture automatique*—especially in terms of the importance placed on the unconscious, which is thought to impose its laws on the writer.[23] Like Surrealist writers André Breton or Paul Éluard, who both let the unconcious dictate sentences to them, Ponge sought to give himself over to things. However, it is the thing's *material substance* that Ponge was interested in; he focused on the material dimension of, for example, bread or a candle. In his notes on water, for instance, he literally imagined water's material substance from the inside, as if he himself had turned into water. And it is only once he attested a special gravity to water that he claimed a quasi-human "hysterical drive" for it.[24] In other words, he argued that water's specific dynamic texture causes it to "behave" like a human being. Ponge aimed to express things "according to their own instructions" and through their "enigmatic fullness."[25] And this devotion to things as they are is more phenomenological than Surrealist. Even when it comes to words, it is not their meaning that stands in the foreground, but their materiality. Ponge considers words to be above all "extraordinary materials."[26] His materialist approach thus extends to words, which he considered to be thinglike: their meaning matters less to him than their material substance.

23 For more on Ponge's discussion about the thing as Other, which dictates its law, see Derrida, *Signéponge/Singnsponge*, 12.

24 Ponge, "Die Kerze," "Das Brot," and "Vom Wasser," in *Im Namen der Dinge*, 13, 21–23, and 41.

25 Ponge, *Schreibpraktiken*, 60, 42.

26 Ponge, 11.

It could be said that in Ponge's work, the materialist-phenomenological approach to things is combined with a Mallarméan sensitivity for the materiality of words.

Things on the Rise

Loosely associated with Surrealist writers like Paulhan or Éluard, Ponge achieved a kind of literary breakthrough with his book *Le parti pris des choses* (The nature of things, 1942). The book was celebrated among his colleagues for privileging the object's perspective.[27] Ponge subsequently received many requests from visual artists to write catalogue texts—they, too, wanted their artworks to be considered in this fashion.[28] Aside from Fautrier, Ponge wrote on artists like Georges Braque, Alberto Giacometti, and Germaine Richier, and the resulting texts were later published in a volume called *L'atelier contemporain* (1977).

One could argue in retrospect that Ponge's *Le parti pris des choses* prompted the more general "turn to things" that was characteristic in French postwar literature. By attempting to bring things to life, Ponge was indeed a precursor to writers like Georges Perec or Alain Robbe-Grillet, because they also aimed to present objects "in and of themselves," "unencumbered by human significance."[29] A focus on things, or rather on objects, was generally on the rise in France after the Second World War. At that time, many writers placed increasing

27 Jean Paulhan writes to Fautrier, for instance, that he considers Ponge's *Le parti pris des choses* to be a "major" work. Paulhan to Fautrier, August 30, 1943, *Fautrier*, 77.

28 Ponge said, "Ceux de peintres et sculpteurs me traitant en familier, eux aussi, au point de souhaiter tout aussitôt se voir traités par moi, à leur tour, je ne dis pas tout à fait comme des choses, mais enfin, à ma manière, c'est sûr." Francis Ponge, "Au lecteur," in *L'atelier contemporain* (Paris: Éditions Gallimard, 1977), vii.

29 See Kristin Ross, *Fast Cars, Clean Bodies: Decolonization and the Reordering of French Culture* (Cambridge, MA: MIT Press, 1995), 2.

importance on objects of a special kind, namely, consumer items.[30] While objects are manifestations of the material world that depend on our perception of them, things seem more autonomous in that they don't presuppose a perceiving subject. As an umbrella term, "things" is also more general and unspecific than the term "objects." Now, we certainly need to relate Ponge's preference for things over humans to the thing- and object-friendly mood of his time. In her seminal book on postwar France, *Fast Cars, Clean Bodies* (1994), Kristin Ross diagnoses a very specific situation in the 1950s in which objects were often seen as more important than people.[31] Although Ponge preferred things over objects—and never explicitly wrote about consumer objects—there are of course structural overlaps between both. Some of the things in particular that he described (e.g., a cigarette or a closet) are also commodities that rely on human labor and take on a value form (commodity Value, to be more precise).[32] But since he projected an almost transcendental power onto these things, it was probably necessary for him to overlook their status as commodities. Sartre actually discussed this possibility: that the reason for Ponge's great belief in things was to be found in his political belief system. For Sartre, there is a correlation between Ponge's tendency to consider things as self-sufficient beings (a belief that is supported by the greater autonomy of things) and his revolutionary belief in a different society.[33] He suggested that Ponge held the view that an autonomous, self-sufficient existence had become impossible in postwar capitalism.

30 Ross, 5.

31 Ross, 177.

32 I discussed the value form of commodities in the chapter "The Economy of Painting" in my book *The Love of Painting*, 316–33.

33 Sartre, "Der Mensch und die Dinge," 6.

But should we really read Ponge's self-sufficient things, like a closet with its "desire to stubbornly stick to the ground,"[34] as allegories for a better, albeit impossible life? Considering that life under capitalism increasingly demanded mobility and flexibility from people (and objects)—objects travel and are exchanged, and people, too, are expected to adapt their changing life conditions and move elsewhere for work—a sedentary existence of an object (like a closet that refuses to move elsewhere) could indeed be desirable. But a weak point in Sartre's allegorical reading of Ponge's writings about things is that he presupposes, in a rather psychologizing fashion, that Ponge himself longed for an existence that was equal to the self-reliant existence of things. Such speculation on personal motivations seems problematic. Sartre went even further in calling Ponge's stones stand-ins for a life that has become petrified, a life that would be dominated by alienation. Ponge set up a similarity between the hard surface of a stone and a hard (difficult) life, inviting us to take one for the other: "Look at the stone, it lives, look at life, it is stone."[35] While his way of animating things could certainly point to a postwar consumer society that lacked vitality, it seems a little reductive to see his stones as critiquing only alienation, because they are described as lifeless *and* full of life. They are said to have "faces" and "bodies"; they laugh, are afraid, and die like human beings, but they are also described as dead objects that are shaped by water and will eventually turn to dust.[36] So instead of metonymically pointing to a hard life, these stones also celebrate life in its fullness. Seen in this light, they could be seen as precursors to

34 Ponge, "Vom Wasser," 41. Ponge writes: "Der Schrank hier zum Beispiel erweist sich als überaus starrköpfig in seinem Verlangen, am Boden zu haften."

35 Sartre, "Der Mensch und die Dinge," 283.

36 See Ponge, "Der Kieselstein," 81–97.

what Bruno Latour later described as *actants* in his actor-network theory: like Ponge's stones, Latour's actants are human and nonhuman hybrids.[37]

Ponge as an Ambivalent Figure

While Ponge's doubly materialist approach to things, words, and his own financial conditions is still topical today, his strong plea for a literature that goes beyond meaning and ideas seems rather questionable.[38] Instead of longing for an (imaginary and fictive) type of writing that abandons meaning production—and that leads, in my opinion, to a weakening of potential in both literature and criticism—one could opt for a type of writing that would be (like Ponge's) sensitive to the material substance of things and words without avoiding the production of meaning or ideas altogether. Ponge is a very inspiring, but also quite problematic, figure. Despite the relevance of his experiments with words and literary forms, especially in times of an often-invoked "crisis of criticism,"[39] Ponge's position toward his female collegues in particular, while reflecting on the misogyny of his time, is unacceptable from today's point of view.

Let's first consider the literary merits of his work. The manifold experiments presented in his book *Pratiques d'écriture* (1984) still seem quite daring. Next to notes about powerful things that are said to be able to "invade" and thus conquer and dominate people,[40] this book contains remarks about the material

37 Bruno Latour, *Das Parlament der Dinge: Für eine politische Ökologie*, trans. Gustav Roßler (Frankfurt am Main: Suhrkamp Verlag, 2009), 155.

38 We often find statements in his writing that argue for a literature without meaning and ideas. One example among many: he proposes that words should be contemplated without taking their meaning into account. Ponge, *Schreibpraktiken*, 11.

39 Sabeth Buchmann and Isabelle Graw, "The Critique of Art Criticism," *Texte zur Kunst*, no. 113 (March 2019): 32–51.

40 Ponge, *Schreibpraktiken*, 19.

substance of words and allusions to Ponge's own financial reasons for having the book published. As well as autofictive writing, Ponge also included different versions of texts, final pieces as well as preliminary drafts and comments that showed his writing process.[41] In a 1943 correspondence with Albert Camus, Ponge stated that writers can only leave "confused notes and dazzling aperçus at this particular historical juncture."[42] In times of crisis (after the Second World War and the Shoah in particular), writers often opt for experimental formats that acknowledge their disorientation. There are moments in history where loose (but splendid) and fragmented observations must be enough. His call for what Deleuze and Guattari would have described as "minor literature" and his encouragement for people to experiment with literary formats resonate today, particularly when the world as we know it undergoes radical changes.[43]

Apart from the undeniable literary merits of Ponge's work, he also held sexist views. His correspondence with Camus is a treasure trove in this respect: both spoke in a discriminatory fashion about their female collegue, the writer Elsa Triolet, whose work they refused to take seriously. Ponge especially lashed out against Triolet's text on Camus, calling it "maternal" and "marked by her sex"; Camus replied that "most women don't think when they write."[44] Ponge discredited her work by

41 See Isabelle Graw and Brigitte Weingart, "Between You and Me: A Correspondence on Autofiction in Contemporary Literature," *Texte zur Kunst*, no. 115 (September 2019): 39–64.

42 Ponge wrote, "Nous laisserons des notes confuses, des aperçus fulgurants, etc." Ponge to Camus, *Correspondance*, 78.

43 My recent book *In Another World: Notes, 2014–2017* (Berlin: Sternberg Press, 2020) contains "notes" and "aperçus" that have been written in times of personal and more general political and social crises.

44 Camus to Ponge, *Correspondance*, 65.

reducing it to gender clichés, and Camus saw this as proof for his assumption that women's writing is devoid of thinking. Another text by Ponge on Germaine Richier is equally full of sexist clichés: the artist is described as a "woman and midwife," and Ponge can't hide his astonishment about the fact that she actually gave birth to artworks, not children.[45] Once again we are reminded here how women artists—owing to their childbearing capabilities—are excluded from the traditonal procreative ideal that imagines only male artists to bear artworks (instead of children). Now the question that arises is, of course, if Ponge's occasional sexist remarks render his doubly materialist approach to things, words, and his own financial conditions irrelevant? Not necessarly. If we consider Ponge as an equally ambivilant and problematic figure, we can still benefit from the formal and theoretical insights of his work.

A Plea for Critics as Friends

At some point in his text on Fautrier, Ponge advised his readers to "listen to these literati gentlemen and friends of the painter." Friends of the artist, presumed to be male, who own paintings given to them by artists, were experts in Ponge's mind.[46] Ponge here alludes to the artist's friends firsthand access to art and to the insider information that results from it. Friends of the artists are ultimately closer to the source, and this is why Ponge advised us to trust their opinion. Rather than idealizing friendships between artists and writers, Ponge also noted how the artist's friends are often condemned to "confused, absurd expressions," while at the same time they have expertise and insider knowledge.[47] Proximity can thus produce both knowledge *and* confusion.

45 Francis Ponge, "Germaine Richier" (1956), *Texte zur Kunst,* 118–22.

46 Ponge, "Bemerkungen zu den 'Geiseln' von Fautrier," 19.

47 Ponge, 20.

As a modus operandi of traditional art writing, friendships between writers and artists are of course not a new phenomenon. Think of early modern art writers like Leon Battista Alberti or André Félibien, who acknowledged friendships with artists whose work they strongly advocated.[48] Today, by contrast, most critical art writers avoid mentioning friendships that might exist with an artist. Neither the privileged access that results from friendship nor the pressure to be loyal to an artist friend is ever discussed. Objections against a friend's practice are also not raised under these circumstances where critical reservation is perceived as an act of disloyality.

Ponge also mentioned the *instrumental* nature of such friendships between artists and writers: he noted how these friendships can also serve the self-interests of those involved in them. While it is certainly true that artists and their writer friends use and benefit from one another, these friendships, according to Ponge, can't be reduced to "self-interest" either. They can also be based on a "vertitable symphathy for one another."[49] Ponge considered such friendships to be contradictory: highly instrumental yet also based on true feelings.

A New Materialism That Doesn't Obscure Its Own Material Conditions

I have already suggested the possibility of Ponge's approach to things as being new materialist avant la lettre. He could even be qualified as a precursor of object-oriented philosophy insofar as he claimed humans to be invaded by things.[50] Like

48 Alberti, "Prolog," in *Della Pittura – Über die Malkunst*, ed. and trans. Oskar Bätschmann and Sandra Gianfreda (Darmstadt: Wissenschaftliche Buchgesellschaft, 2002), 63; and Félibien, preface to *Entretiens sur les vies et sur les ouvrages des plus excellens peintres anciens et modernes* (Paris, 1886).

49 Ponge, "Bemerkungen zu den 'Geiseln' von Fautrier," 19.

50 Ponge, *Schreibpraktiken*, 19.

new materialism, he assumed a materiality that is self-active; for example, oranges are said to have an "attitude," and a splint basket is said to be "puzzled," because it was put in the rubbish.[51] The language Ponge uses—from describing oranges or Fautrier's "Hostages" paintings—is quite animistic. He described paintings mutating into "faces" that become dark from their own blood (and impressions caused by the blood sensation of pigment). He also considered them to be "cramped, ripped apart, and mutilated bodies that are eaten up by flies." Fautrier's paintings are not considered portraits that represent suffering, and they don't depict physical terror (namely, the torture methods the Nazis used against innocent people during occupation), but they *are* "cadavers, these crushed faces."[52] The animistic tendency of his writing is most pronounced in his collection of prose poems *Le parti pris des choses,* where inanimate things, like stones or shells, are literally brought to life.

When writing about a cigarette, for instance, he described it as a person.[53] However, while rendering these things alive, he also hinted to the projective nature of his vitalist operations. In the text about the cigarette, he wrote: "Let's first speak about its equally hazy, dry, and disheveled atmosphere." The presence of a beholding subject is acknowledged here—its presence being necessary for things to be perceived as living beings.

This is true for Fautrier's "Hostages" paintings as well: for them to be perceived literally as bleeding heads, someone like Ponge had to describe them that way. Ponge's materialism is

51 Ponge, 13.
52 Ponge, 30.
53 Ponge, "Die Zigarette," in *Im Namen der Dinge*, 15.

one that acknowledges the importance of the projecting subject for things to come to life, which is something new materialism tends not to do. But while anthropomorphizing Fautrier's paintings, Ponge also reminded us how they are in fact paintings, paintings that consists of dead matter, a matter he discussed in detail. At one point in the text, he described how Fautrier applied color with thick strokes.[54] So apart from Ponge's vitalistic projections on Fautrier's work, he managed to grasp their material specificity as well.

But in his writing on Fautrier, he also never lets us forget that the "liveliness" suggested in these paintings is an effect of specific material procedures. And unlike most critics today, Ponge reflects on his own material (financial and social) conditions as something that not only reaches deep into his writing, but also affects the form his writing takes.

54 Ponge, "Bemerkungen zu den 'Geiseln' von Fautrier," 31.

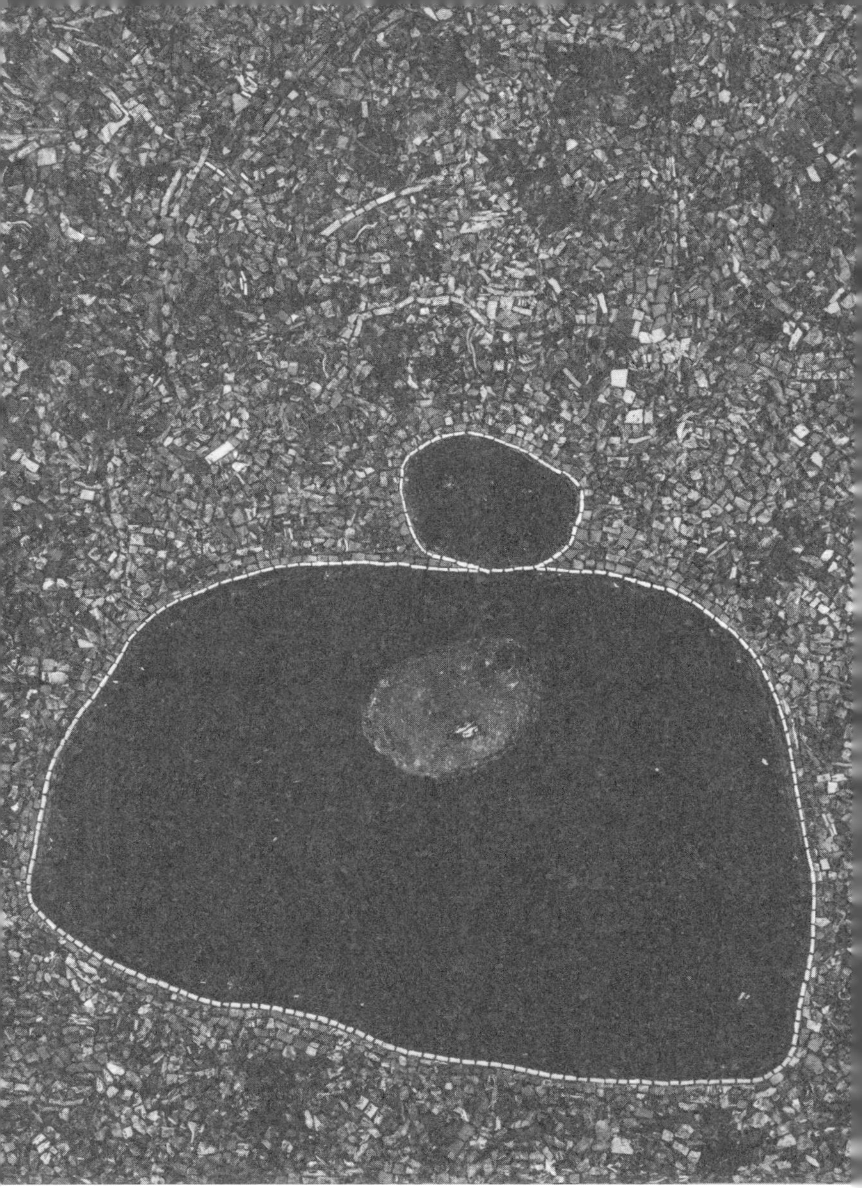

Jack Whitten, *Black Monolith X, (The Birth of Muhammad Ali)*, 2016

Animated Gifts in the Exchange System
Reflections on Jack Whitten's Paintings[1]

Animated Material

In Jack Whitten's work, the suggestive forces of the material—rather than ideas—are foregrounded. The fact that he has repeatedly (and vehemently) distanced himself from Conceptual art, or more precisely from a traditional understanding of Conceptual art as an idea- and concept-based form of artistic practice is, in my view, also related to his focus on the inherent forces of his materials.[2] And in line with new materialism, Whitten sees matter as something powerful rather than as a mute, disposable mass.[3] However, for his material to come across as "animated," certain methods of aesthetic production are required as well as an observer who is able to animate the material in his or her mind—two factors that are often not prioritized in new materialism.

In Whitten's memorial paintings—produced after 1968 and the focus of his 2019 exhibition at Hamburger Bahnhof, Berlin—this interplay of suggestive material, vitality effects, and

1 Written on the occasion of the exhibition "Jack Whitten: Jack's Jacks" at Hamburger Bahnhof, Berlin, March 29–September 1, 2019.

2 See some of Whitten's remarks regarding this in Katy Siegel, ed., *Jack Whitten: Notes from the Woodshed* (Zurich: Hauser & Wirth, 2018). A 1984 entry states: "I must be careful not to depend upon conceptual thought" (174). Or an entry from 1986: "I don't believe in Conceptual art; if you can conceive of it then it's not art but an illustration of an idea" (190). Or: "I must work against Sol LeWitt. Saw the ACE Gallery Show, 100% conceptual. Work against the conceptual" (233).

3 In an interview with Jeanne Siegel, Whitten commented on his painting *Black Monolith III (For Barbara Jordan)* (1998): "I'm beginning to see that there's a relation here when I speak of spirit and matter. That it is possible to direct something into matter. Congresswoman Barbara Jordan is my next subject. You see that bucket over there? She's in that bucket! I have to put her in there through the spirit." Quoted in Jeanne Siegel, *Painting after Pollock: Structures of Influence* (Amsterdam: G&B Arts International, 1999), 40.

vitalistic projection can be traced more precisely. A variety of methods is evident in this body of paintings, starting with the titles and their dedicatory character (such as *Clocking for Stanley Kubrick*, 1999), to the relief-like surfaces made of colorful acrylic pieces, up to the way the emphasized working process with which Whitten, who died in 2018, was able to "ensoul" his paintings, transforming them into quasi-spiritual objects. In my opinion, the fact that Whitten's memorial paintings per their titles appear as *gifts* for mostly deceased people contributes to their "animated-ness" as well, as much as their color surfaces, which almost seem to transport the soul of the deceased. In addition, the paintings often show toolmarks on their surfaces, thus vitalizing them and directly augmenting them with something of the artist's lifetime and working time. Given this, it is not only a question of working out exactly *how* Whitten succeeds in vitalizing his works (i.e., with what artistic methods). For his work to be perceived as animated, certain methods of aesthetic production need to be interwoven with an animistic reception. However, there are also sociohistorical reasons *why* the material plays an active, vital role in Whitten's work. I would argue that the specific charge of his material leads to an impression of "soulfulness" in his works, and that this symbolically advances their circulation in the art system.

Sculptures as Blueprints

Whitten cut his material—or more precisely, acrylic paint—into small pieces and placed them onto the surface of the canvas, giving the paintings a mosaiclike impression; they thus appear object-like and their surfaces rough and choppy. In my view, it is the aesthetic principles seen in his wooden sculptures (unfortunately these were not shown in the Hamburger Bahnhof exhibition) that are revisited and driven forward in the memorial paintings.[4] These rarely shown sculptures—hybrids of African sculpture, folk art, and Cycladic objects—provide the blueprint for his paintings. Some of them, for example, have nails on their surfaces, a nod to *minkisi* sculptures of Central Africa, which were likewise studded with nails and functioned as containers for supernatural forces. Whitten's objects also appear to possess magical power. The nail principle in the sculptures is taken up and modified in his paintings via the cut pieces of colored acrylic, which he referred to as tesserae. In a film included in the exhibition, Whitten can be seen sticking the tesserae onto the surface with a pointed object, rendering dots on the surfaces of some of the small stones. Like the nails, these irregularly cut elements also provide a powerful, dynamic surface. In any case, it is in Whitten's tesserae work that the potential for vitality traditionally associated with color enters a new phase, with the three-dimensional color pieces enhancing the sensual/haptic quality of the color even further. In the monumental painting dedicated to Prince, *Quantum Wall (A Gift for Prince)* (2016)—its purple tones in keeping with Prince's best-known song, "Purple Rain"—the three-dimensionality of the color pieces leads to the impression of a dazzling polychromatism that can change depending on where the viewer stands. Likewise, the objects and patterns on the surface of the painting *Ode to Andy: For Andy Warhol* (1986) take inspiration from that found in the living world, such as stones, fish, and a silver metal plate, the latter alluding directly to Andy Warhol's Silver Factory. Via the metal plate, a surplus reference to a specific life-world seems to enter the painting. Unlike collage or assemblage works that often use imagery found in everyday

4 See the catalogue that focuses on his sculptures, *Odyssey: Jack Whitten Sculpture, 1963–2017* (New York: Metropolitan Museum of Art, 2018).

life directly, such references in Whitten's work are mediated by color. Once again, it is Whitten's material (color) that always retains the upper hand as the medium of impression: in Whitten's work, color serves above all to represent the people honored in the titles of his works. It is not so much a carrier of expression; rather, its function is symbolic.

The dedicatory character of his memorial paintings can also be found in the sculptures. In this context, we can simply think of Whitten's anthropomorphic *John Lennon Altarpiece* (1968), studded with nails, or *The Guardian II, For Mirsini* (1984), an object of protection for his family. Through their dedications, the titles of these works function as paratexts, ensuring that each gift recipient or remembered or honored person remains present in the object itself. We can take Whitten's Muhammad Ali painting, *Black Monolith X, (The Birth of Muhammad Ali)* (2016), which is part of his "Black Monolith" series (1988–2017), as another example of how the memory of a person literally enters into the color and morphology of his paintings. At the lower end of a typical Whitten field of glued-on and cut-off color pieces, there is a black, oval, crusty, and Dubuffet-esque form that brings the figure of the absent Muhammad Ali directly into play, as if he were risen from the debris-like ground of the image. By evoking the birth of Muhammad Ali, the title of this painting recalls his self-directed transformation from champion boxer Cassius Clay to athlete-cum-civil-rights-activist, a kind of rebirth, and one to which the abstract pictorial language of this painting clearly alludes.

Titles as Vivification Devices

It is, then, primarily the titles of Whitten's images that have a vivifying effect. *The Messenger: For Art Blakey* (1990), for example, is a title that honors both the legendary jazz drummer Art Blakey and his band, the Messengers. The drummer's almost extraterrestrial ability is captured in the cosmic atmosphere of this black-and-white grid, which from a distance resembles a universe densely populated with stars. It could be said that every memorial painting preserves what Whitten saw as the essence of the artistic or political achievement of the person honored in its title.

In Whitten's work, painting and title often stand in a metonymic relationship to one another: the meaning of the one is usually found in the other. So instead of producing a gap between the meaning suggested in the title and what the image presents us with visually—as is often the case, for example, in Dadaist or neo-Dadaist paintings—with Whitten we are usually confronted with correspondences: with the help of an abstract visual language, that with which the title is associated is confirmed in the image. Whitten's black, largely monochrome painting *Sweet Little Angel, For B. B. King* (2015) is a fine example of this, with its neon-sprayed string on its surface that represents a guitar string. The fact that Whitten's paintings so often use an abstract visual language to depict that which is proclaimed in their titles may at times be read as somewhat redundant, too obvious. At the same time, however, the titles charge the paintings they name with a specific history of time and culture.

In addition to numerous jazz musicians, Whitten also paid tribute to several—mostly male—visual artists in his memorial paintings, first and foremost among these being his friend and mentor Norman Lewis, that influential pioneer of abstract painting to whom Whitten's monumental *Norman Lewis Triptych I* (1985) is dedicated.

One's Own Role Models

In the 1950s, Norman Lewis was the only African American painter to participate in the "artists' sessions" organized by Franz Kline and Willem de Kooning at Studio 35 in New York.[5] However, he was consistently erased by the official historiographies, as in the texts of Clement Greenberg, Harold Rosenberg, and Irving Sandler.[6] In this context, the monumental dimensions of Whitten's painting *Norman Lewis Triptych I* can even be read as a kind of correction of the canon. Lewis's emblematic and calligraphic-seeming pictorial language, however, is willfully both synthesized and broken down into its components. For example, it is the colorfulness rather than the conspicuous vertical structure of Lewis's painting *Untitled* (1949), a triptych that recalls Mondrian, that Whitten transforms into a grid structure on a black background in his own painting. Alongside Lewis, de Kooning was another major inspiration for Whitten, as can be felt in numerous gestural paintings from the 1960s, such as *King's Wish (Martin Luther's Dream)* (1968), and in the title of his seemingly photographic grid painting *Bill's Way: For de Kooning* (1989).[7] In the latter homage, it is above all the broad brushstrokes and skin colors typical

5 See the preface and acknowledgments in Norman L. Kleeblatt and Stephen Brown, eds., *From the Margins: Lee Krasner/Norman Lewis, 1945–1952* (New York: Jewish Museum, 2014), 11–13.

6 See Mia L. Bagneris, "Loner in the Dark: The Singular Vision of Norman Lewis and the Evidence of Things Unseen," in Kleeblatt and Brown, *From the Margins*, 81.

7 For Whitten's remark that "Abstract Expressionism was my academy," see Jack Whitten, interview by Judith Olch Richards, December 1–3, 2009, transcript, Archives of American Art, The Smithsonian, https://www.aaa.si.edu/collections/interviews/oral-history-interview-jack-whitten-15748#overview.

of de Kooning that Whitten literally dissect and analyze with the help of a grid structure, thereby also immobilizing their effect.

It would be insufficient to comprehend his memorial paintings solely as a confrontation with various superegos or as an instance of Harold Bloom's much-quoted "anxiety of influence." On the contrary, they also bear witness to the existential necessity for a Black artist in the New York of the late 1960s, the 1970s, and the 1980s, who was also an abstract painter, who sought out *his own role models* (also from jazz) because of a lack of recognition and encouragement.[8] Jazz musicians honored in his paintings—such as John Coltrane or Bud Powell—ultimately represent the success story of that art form, to which Whitten then ties his references. Within the history of painting there had still not been a comparable rise to prominence for Black artists. Whitten was also confronted with a double exclusion: first, around 1971, his politically committed colleagues considered it to be "hugely unfashionable" to paint in a nonrepresentative manner;[9] second, the majority of art institutions and the art market, which is still today dominated by white actors, was largely closed off to him for a very long time.[10] Whitten, who was forced for many years to earn his living as a teacher, found the debates and discussions with his students to be enormously important. Nevertheless, he did not correspond to the clichéd image of the obsessive painter-

8 In the abovementioned interview, Whitten once again stated how no one gave him support: "There was no encouragement from nobody." And on the 1970s, he said: "The idea of a black abstract artist doing those works and thinking that way, nobody paid attention to you." Whitten, interview by Richards.

9 See Darby English, *1971: A Year in the Life of Color* (Chicago: University of Chicago Press, 2016), 73.

10 In 2012, Whitten said: "I have survived with very little help from the 'artworld,' the white artworld simply denies my existence." Quoted in Siegel, *Jack Whitten*, 392.

genius who devotes his or her time exclusively to painting.[11] That Whitten necessarily had to approach his heroes of postwar art—such as Andy Warhol, Cy Twombly, and Ellsworth Kelly—from the outside because of his social marking as a "Black artist" is made clear in paintings such as the homage to Kelly, *One Hundred Ninety Pieces of Color: For Ellsworth Kelly #2* (2016), an image in which Whitten's distinct approach to modernism is formally echoed. Kelly's predilection for ready-made colors is built on here in the form of colorful, glossy clusters of paint pressed directly from the tube. But Kelly's impersonal recourse to commercial color charts has been replaced by a physical process of pressing that moreover results in pure material. Unlike Kelly, who sought to minimize the sensual potential of color, Whitten's Kelly homage demonstrates the haptic and vivifying effect of color that is central to Whitten's work. He thus refers to Kelly's method in a way that captures and, in so doing, transcends its exemplary character.

Even when Whitten appropriates the modernist topos of the grid, his position as being "from the margins" is always latently in operation.[12] Or, to go even further, in his variations on this motif, the modernist myth of the grid is taken, ad absurdum, as a guarantor of "flatness." This is the case in *Totem VI Annunciation: For John Coltrane* (2000), for example, a multipart work that features clusters of mostly grayish pieces of acrylic paint. Both these color pieces and the grid formations they make up appear extremely crooked and slanted. As in jazz, Whitten has used a strictly formal model (the grid) to simultaneously

11 This was also due to the painting breaks Whitten took in the summer, during which he exclusively produced his wooden sculptures on Crete.

12 "From the Margins" was the title of the aforementioned Lee Krasner and Norman Lewis exhibition at the Jewish Museum in New York from 2014 to 2015.

liberate himself from it. Omnipresent in his work are grids that appear organic, that curve, or whose outer forms have been rounded off, as evidenced by images such as *Yankee Clipper: For Joe DiMaggio* (1999) and *Quantum Wall, VIII (For Arshile Gorky, My First Love in Painting)* (2017). When Whitten takes the liberty in these works of producing crooked and slanted grids, it signals two things: that the tradition of the grid is not something he can take for granted, and that the modernist claim of the grid to overcome the figure-ground relation does not reach far enough. Whitten's grids do not create the impression of flatness; rather, they suggest a three-dimensional, bodily form of vitality.

Traces of Doing It Yourself

Alongside the titles, the color pieces, and things cast with paint, visible traces of work in Whitten's oeuvre also ensure that his work is symbolically enriched with something of its creator's lifetime and the period in which he worked. In his seemingly graphical target painting *Red Black Green* (1979–80) and in the painting *Zulu Tea Parlor* (1973), with "wounds" on its surface, clear tool marks give evidence of Whitten's working process. On the surface of *Red Black Green*, for example, the paint has been spread horizontally with an Afro comb. In *Zulu Tea Parlor*, one of Whitten's homemade notched squeegees has torn visible stripes into the surface. It is therefore not only an inscription of "events or persons into the material of the paint itself" (as per curator Sven Beckstette) that takes place in these paintings; the paintings also bear witness to Whitten's specific working method.[13] The fact that Whitten liked to resort to self-made or unconventional tools—such as giant

13 See Sven Beckstette, "Die Bedeutung der Abstraktion erweitern," in *Jack Whitten: Jack's Jacks*, ed. Udo Kittelmann and Sven Beckstette (Berlin: Hamburger Bahnhof, 2019), 51.

squeegees (he called them "developers," in reference to photographic processes), Afro combs, planes, saws, and wall trowels—articulates first and foremost the do-it-yourself character of his method. These tools are not only a means to an end; they are significant in themselves, which is why Whitten occasionally presented them in his exhibitions (such as at the Daniel Newburg Gallery in New York in 1994).

The peculiarity of these tools seems to lie largely in the fact that they bring about both mechanization and an idiosyncratic form of personalization of his working method. With the Afro comb, for example, the significance of the hand is emphasized and the painterly process mechanized, while at the same time the use of the comb highlights the more personal and political themes present in his work. Similarly, the monumental, self-made squeegee Whitten used to produce his so-called slab paintings in one go (e.g., *Zulu Tea Parlor*) does not merely perform the mechanization of the working process, but also performs its individualization. With the squeegee, Whitten ultimately informs us that artists must do everything themselves if they are not clearly embedded in the (characteristically Eurocentric and racist) tradition of painting. At the same time, the squeegee also signals Whitten's affiliation to postwar modernism, in which squeegees were common tools used by artists such as Ed Clark, K. O. Götz, and Gerhard Richter. Whitten had in fact always claimed such modernity as a matter of course, typified by his declaration in the title of one of his images that the painter Arshile Gorky was his "first love in painting."

The Obligation to Reciprocate

As suggested above, it seems to me that there remains an essential connection between the "dedicatory character" of Whitten's memorial paintings and the proposition of their animateness (by way of color, title, color imprints, and traces of work). That Whitten characterized his paintings as "gifts to the people who inspired them" can help point us in the right direction: according to the anthropologist Marcel Mauss, gifts cannot so easily be removed from the sphere of economy and exchange.[14] By examining forms of exchange in various non-Western societies, Mauss has shown that gifts are animate objects of exchange rather than inanimate ones. Once a gift has been received, something must be returned on the assumption that a piece of their giver lives on within the gift. According to this, gifts are part of a perpetual economic cycle. Whitten then modifies this animistic principle to the effect that it is the soul of the recipient, rather than the soul of the giver, that his memorial paintings contain. And it is precisely because his paintings also function as quasi-magical ritual objects that they must, per Mauss, be exchanged. From this anthropological perspective, one could then interpret the gift structure of Whitten's paintings as an attempt to force entry into the economic cycle of the art market. Or, to put it another way, by presenting the paintings as gifts—to Robert Rauschenberg, for example, as in the digital-looking *Bar Code IV Lotto (A Gift for Robert Rauschenberg)* (2008), or to Louise Bourgeois, as in *Saint Louise AKA The Tittie Painting for Louise Bourgeois* (2010), which regrettably reproduces sexist clichés—they also participate in an exchange system that marginalized them for

14 Whitten, quoted in Siegel, *Notes from the Woodshed*, 418. See also Marcel Mauss, *The Gift: The Form and Reason for Exchange in Archaic Societies*, trans. W. D. Halls (London: Routledge, 1990).

such a long time. In the 1970s, Whitten himself is said to have been indignant about the fact that his paintings were sold below their artistic and monetary value.[15] With these manifold methods to animate his paintings, he took the risk to deviate from the ideal of a series of mechanically produced works with the appearance of lifelessness (as aspired to by Minimalism and Pop art). At the same time, however, it was via the very dedication of his paintings to artist colleagues that he found a place in the postwar canon. The fact that Whitten's paintings now have institutional recognition and increasing market value is also owing to structural reasons (such as the long-overdue commitment of numerous art institutions to "diversity") and, consequently, cannot be attributed solely to the animistic potential of his works. Nevertheless, I believe that the various methods of animating them, including their presentation as gifts, have been symbolically conducive to their circulation and interchangeability.

With reference to Samo Tomšič's critique of vitalism, one could question the extent to which we are dealing with a "positive vitalism" in Whitten's case (in the form of vivifying titles, materials suggestive of aliveness, and animated gifts), where "negativity" falls by the wayside.[16] First and foremost, however, negativity seems to me an attitude (or procedure) not every artist can afford. As long as artists and their works are discriminated against because of skin color, for instance, positive-vitalistic self-assertion may be more urgently required than negativity. And if one understands the majority of

15 See Zoé Whitley, "Brotherliness: Melvin Edwards Reflects on 50 Years of Friendship with Jack Whitten," in Kittelmann and Beckstette, *Jack Whitten*, 136.

16 See Samo Tomšič, *The Labour of Enjoyment: Towards a Critique of Libidinal Economy* (Cologne: August Verlag, 2019), 204.

Whitten's memorial paintings as a kind of cult of the dead, then the absence of the honored could actually be interpreted as a sign of negativity. The strength of Whitten's positive vitalism seems to me to lie in the fact that it is not the artist himself who is celebrated as something quasi living, but rather his social-artistic system of reference. Whitten himself is to some extent declared to be part of this vital structure; the others are thus always implicated in his "I."

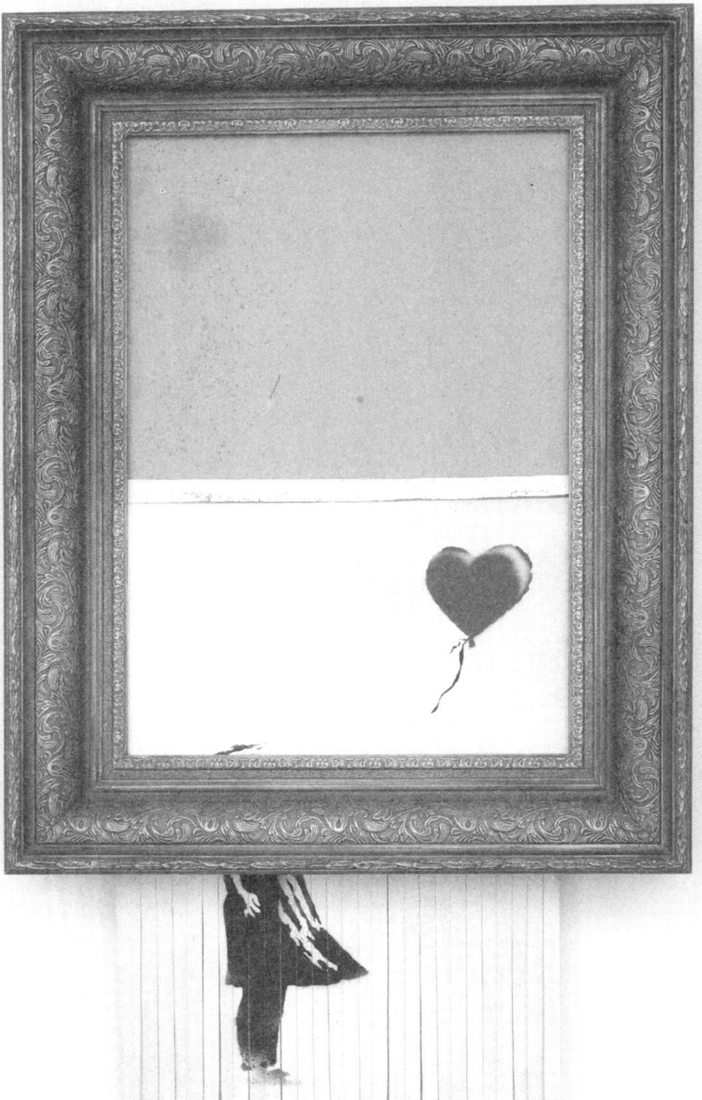

A Value-Theoretical Banksy

Just after being auctioned at Sotheby's on October 5, 2018, Banksy's work *Girl with Balloon* (2006) was partially shredded by a mechanism that had been built into its frame. This act, carefully planned and executed by Banksy and his studio, as demonstrated in a 2018 video, *Shred the Love: The Director's Cut,* was much discussed in the media at the time, with reports appearing on the evening news and in celebrity magazines. In early 2019, *Girl with Balloon* was presented with its new title, *Love Is in the Bin* (2018), at Museum Frieder Burda in Baden-Baden, where it was celebrated as an icon. The artwork was later on loan for a year in the Staatsgalerie Stuttgart, where the curators presented it like a precious masterpiece behind bullet-proof glass. In light of these recent institutional valorizations, it seems necessary to examine the special value form of this work and its art-historical significance.

Theoretical Premises

Artworks, and thus also Banksy's *Love Is in the Bin,* have a *special value form* that differentiates them from other goods. Although the commodity Value of artworks and of ordinary goods can both be traced back to a form of labor that also may be *immaterial* if it takes the form of ideas, concepts, or communication, artworks—as distinct from other goods—are capable of suggesting the presence of an *artistic labor* (that is in truth absent). Unlike ordinary commodities, in which the work expended on them remains largely hidden, artworks give the impression that they contain the very artistic labor on

Left: Banksy, *Love Is in the Bin*, 2018

which they are determined. Works of art nourish, in other words, the (vitalistic) idea that their Value has physical substance. This, however, is a *materially induced* idea, and one that does not arise by chance. Artworks trigger this vitalist notion, not only by giving it a material vehicle, but also by intervening concretely in their respective social contexts in a specific way. The illusory belief in art's intrinsic value is thus directly related to the structural idiosyncrasies of artworks. In contrast to serially produced luxury goods, artworks are material one-offs,[1] each one ascribed to a singular author. It is the signature that directly links this product back to its author, such that it is associated with their comparatively privileged artistic labor. Although artistic labor is established as the blueprint for creative work, the former involves a far greater degree of self-determination. Economic constraints, such as imposed deadlines to deliver artworks for art fairs or collectors asking for changes to be made to the work, may enter into the artist's studio, but artists can still largely determine their own working hours and the content and purpose of their products: the creative worker in an advertising agency can only dream of the freedom associated with artistic labor. In contrast to an artist, he or she has no claim of ownership on the unique material product that results from this labor. If the artist produces art in the traditional sense, he or she as the author can present a material product as the result of the work that belongs to him or her, at least until it is sold and changes hands. And these privileges associated with artistic work resonate conversely in the material product of art.

1 This even applies to immaterial works such as performances—relics, props, or video documentation ensure the presence of a material vehicle to which their value can be attached.

However, the special value form of an artwork is not only founded on the specificity of artistic labor; it is also dependent on its reception. For the specific intervention of a work of art in its context to be considered significant (i.e., symbolically valuable), a collective, affective force—one the French economist André Orléan calls *affect commun*—must be directed toward it.[2] And this receptive power, which functions mimetically, per Orléan, invests itself only in certain objects, such that others can be left behind. For an artwork to be associated with Value, certain conditions in terms of production aesthetics (solidifying it as a material, long-lasting, one-off product of privileged artistic labor) must be present, as do the receptive forces that desire it.

Girl with Balloon as a Thing of Value

Taking this value-theory proposition as a springboard, it could be said that Banksy's painting *Girl with Balloon* had already fulfilled the essential prerequisites for the genesis of art's special value form, even before its highly publicized shredding. Both the uniqueness principle (so essential for the special value form of art) and materiality were present, the latter in the form of acrylic on canvas. According to Sotheby's, this image represents a rare example of a Banksy original, even despite the fact that its motif, seemingly very popular with Banksy fans, has previously circulated as graffiti.[3] From a value-theoretical perspective, the fact that this motif stems from graffiti gives it "street credibility." Or, to speak in terms of reception theory: being anchored in a graffiti milieu, the frisson of illegal activity can be projected onto this image. With its formal language, *Girl with Balloon* demonstrates the signature Banksy style of

2 André Orléan, *The Empire of Value: A New Foundation for Economics*, trans. M. B. DeBevoise (Cambridge, MA: MIT Press, 2014).

3 Martin Bull, *This Is Not a Photo Opportunity: The Street Art of Banksy* (Oakland, CA: PM Press, 2015), 169.

the early 2000s, which was stenciled by Banksy (or one of his employees) rather than painted with a free hand.[4] And despite Banksy's much-vaunted anonymity, it is nevertheless attributed to him. The pervasive nexus that underlies art's special value form—that of material product and singular creator—likewise asserts itself here. Post-avant-garde attempts to question authorship have not, in truth, managed to undermine the author principle, which has on the contrary been reformatted and expanded. According to Banksy's dealer, there is a buzz created by factors such as his anonymity,[5] which makes a positive contribution to the valorization process. Art's Value is stimulated by such narratives; this has been the case since the early modern era, when equivalent legends and anecdotes about artists drove the process of value attribution.

The spray-painted visual motif—and especially its off-white, foggy, "painterly" background—also suggest *Girl with Balloon* can be traced back to artistic labor. This image thus nourishes the central (vitalistic) notion of value creation: that the artist's absent, tangible labor is somehow present in it. Its Value once again appears to have substance. However, the work stored within *Girl with Balloon* (apparently) ranges from specifically artistic to general work, further increasing its ability to fascinate, in my opinion. On the one hand, Banksy has long operated as an entrepreneurial artist who successfully sells prints and gadgets on his website.[6] It is no coincidence that the name Banksy contains the word "bank"—it seems that he

4 "Banksy doesn't actually execute a lot of the street art pieces anymore." Will Ellsworth-Jones, *Banksy: The Man behind the Wall* (New York: St. Martins Press, 2012), 179.

5 According to Will Ellsworth-Jones, "His anonymity creates a buzz." Ellworth-Jones, *Man behind the Wall*, 104.

6 Robert Clarke describes Banksy as a "corporate artist" who circulates screen prints, canvas paintings, stickers, and books as exhibition concepts. Robert Clarke, *Seven Years with Banksy* (London: Michael O'Mara, 2012), 61.

humorously identifies himself with the workings of a financial institution.

At the same time, however, and in contrast to an entrepreneur, Banksy also behaves like a rule-breaking anarchist artist who spray-paints buildings to rebel against property ownership.[7] The freedoms and violation of rules that are granted to him as a graffiti artist enter into a perfect symbiosis with the model of the *corporate artist*, once again proving that subversive rebellion can be easily marketed under capitalism.

Simplistic Value Reflection

Viewed more generously, *Girl with Balloon* could also be described as a work that addresses its own Value, doing so (sadly) in a decidedly facile manner. The old-master styling of the image's framing can be read as a (richly trivial) symbol for the symbolic value-increasing crossover from graffiti to the sphere of high art and auction. His infantile, easy-to-grasp iconography—the flying red balloon in the shape of a heart, with the figure of a child reaching for it in vain—could also allude to a Value that is similarly impossible to capture owing to its relational and metonymic character, as described by Karl Marx. Like a balloon that is full of air and could burst at any time, Value, too, is built on sand. We could also read this visual scene as a deliberately banal allegory of unrequited love, since the object of love here eludes desire. In its trivial symbolism, this heart communicates formally and aesthetically with Jeff Koons's *Hanging Heart* (1994–2006), which also set an auction record in 2007. At the same time, however, *Girl with Balloon* also seems to make fun of art collectors who take such works

7 See Simon Hattenstone's interview with Banksy, "Something to Spray," *Guardian*, July 17, 2003, https://www.theguardian.com/artanddesign/2003/jul/17/art.artsfeatures.

(whether by Koons or Banksy) seriously and spend serious amounts of money on them. Banksy's previous work *Morons (White and Gold)* (2006) presents an auction scene, with an antique-framed picture with the words: "I can't believe you morons actually buy this shit." From this "speaking" image, it is the artist who seems to turn himself to his auction audience, who he insults in an *épater le bourgeois*–like manner ("you morons"), who will of course then adore him in return.

Value Destruction as Value Creation

How can the act of shredding be interpreted in terms of value theory? According to Banksy, the shredding mechanism built into the work was meant to destroy the painting completely, but, as is well known, did not succeed. However, such artist statements are questionable and should not be taken at face value. But in terms of value theory, it makes a considerable difference whether this picture's materiality is completely destroyed or whether its central motif, the heart, remains visible, as it still is in the shredded image of the girl. Despite the partial destruction of the canvas, *Love Is in the Bin* still ensures that Value can be attached to a tangible, material vehicle. And going even further, the image elements shredded into strips function as relics of an act that is now integrated into the work—like a form of surplus value. After the first shock was overcome, the auction house was able to proudly announce that the Banksy work was the first work of art to have been produced during an auction. The fact that it carries within it an act of apparent destruction of Value—an act that attracted worldwide attention—means that it has now become an icon. Its market value is also said to have risen enormously since the auction.[8]

8 See Anny Shaw, "Banksy Seller's Stringent Instruction for Sotheby's Revealed," *The Art Newspaper*, October 17, 2018, https://www.theartnewspaper.com/news/banksy-sale-stipulations.

The media spectacle, however, formed a striking contrast to attitudes in art history and art criticism that continue to shun the Banksy phenomenon. Accordingly, there is very little serious writing on him. The market success of this work also proves that skepticism about Banksy's artistic significance carries little weight in the auction room. Orléan's collective desire, which is directed only at certain works of art, is clearly not to be understood as a uniformity, but as something split within itself. And in certain segments of the art world, such as the secondary market, the opinion of art experts carries less weight than that of collectors, agents, and the media. Has Banksy's act caused a credibility problem for auction houses? Yes and no. It was possible to sense a kind of Banksy effect in the short term, with many lots in the following auctions unexpectantly not receiving bids (such as works by Christopher Wool, Lucio Fontana, and John Baldessari); perhaps the sight of the partially destroyed canvas cast a lingering doubt among bidders as to the supposed intrinsic value of artworks. At the same time, however, Banksy's act also reveals the limits of a subversive act in which the artist, via his picture, infiltrates the auction sphere as a voluntaristic subject in order to outsmart it. Banksy's attempt to withdraw the Value of its material basis led, foreseeably, to an expansion of its Value. The manifold artistic attempts at destroying the symbolic, market, or commodity value of their work that have taken place throughout the history of art have always proved to generate more Value;[9] what is interesting about Banksy's act, however, is that

9 One of many examples of the expansion of the zone of value described here would be John Baldessari's legendary *Cremation Project* (1970), where the burning of his pictures produced a relic of the act—an urn with ashes. There are also documentary photos of the act, providing a material vehicle for its value. The burning of his images also represented the originary scene of his conceptual approach and, for art history, one of his most significant actions.

it remains within the value sphere instead of aiming at an imaginary point located beyond it, as artists often do today. But instead of subversively infiltrating the sphere of value like Banksy, thus overestimating the artist's authority and underestimating the structure of value formation, it would, in my opinion, be more fruitful to see yourself as part of a context of different values, the norms of which you simultaneously question by way of a (fictitious) distance. In this way, the values and norms of this sphere could become destabilized, perhaps even losing their validity in the long term.

Isabelle Graw is the publisher of the journal *Texte zur Kunst*, which she cofounded with Stefan Germer (1958–1998) in 1990, and professor of art history and art theory at the Hochschule für Bildende Künste – Städelschule, Frankfurt am Main. Her previous books include *In Another World: Notes, 2014–2017* (2020), *The Love of Painting: Genealogy of a Success Medium* (2018), *High Price: Art Between the Market and Celebrity Culture* (2010), and *Die bessere Hälfte: Künstlerinnen des 20. und 21. Jahrhunderts* (2003). Graw lives in Berlin.

14: Jean Fautrier, *Tete d'Otage no. 1* (*Head of a Hostage no. 1*), 1944. Mixed media on paper mounted on linen, 34.93 × 27.31 cm. Courtesy of the Museum of Contemporary Art, Los Angeles, The Panza Collection. © VG Bild-Kunst, Bonn 2020.

32: Jack Whitten, *Black Monolith X, (The Birth of Muhammad Ali)*, 2016. Acrylic on canvas, 213 × 160 × 7.5 cm. © Jack Whitten Estate. Courtesy of the Jack Whitten Estate and Hauser & Wirth. Photo: John Berens.

46: Banksy, *Love Is in the Bin*, 2018. Photo: picture alliance/Photoshot.

Isabelle Graw
Three Cases of Value Reflection
Ponge, Whitten, Banksy

Series editors: Isabelle Graw, Daniel Birnbaum, Institut für Kunstkritik, Hochschule für Bildende Künste – Städelschule, Frankfurt am Main
Series concept: Isabelle Graw
Publisher: Sternberg Press

© 2020 Isabelle Graw, the editors, Sternberg Press
All rights reserved, including the right of reproduction in whole or in part in any form.

Inside dust jacket: Eliza Douglas, *Untitled*, 2020. Oil on canvas, 210 × 160 cm.
Photo: Marc Domage. Courtesy of the artist and Air de Paris, Paris.

Managing editor: Niamh Dunphy
Proofreading: Raphael Wolf
Translation (DE–EN): Matthew Scown (Jack Whitten and Banksy texts)
Design: Anna Landskron and Marie Bader, Surface, Berlin/Frankfurt am Main

Printing: Tallinn Book Printers
Dust jacket: Munken Print White, 1.5 vol., 150 gsm
Cover: Zanders Efalin fine linen, 280 gsm
Inside: Munken Print Cream, 1.5 vol., 115 gsm
Typeface: Arno Pro; Akzidenz-Grotesk BQ

ISBN 978-3-95679-525-1

Distributed by The MIT Press, Art Data, and Les presses du réel

Sternberg Press
Caroline Schneider
Karl-Marx-Allee 78
D-10243 Berlin
www.sternberg-press.com